Sea Turtles

by Martha E. H. Rustad

Consulting Editor: Gail Saunders-Smith, Ph.D.

Consultant: Jody Byrum, Science Writer,
SeaWorld Education Department

Pebble Books

an imprint of Capstone Press
Mankato, Minnesota

Pebble Books are published by Capstone Press
151 Good Counsel Drive, P.O. Box 669, Mankato, Minnesota 56002
http://www.capstone-press.com

1 2 3 4 5 6 06 05 04 03 02 01

Library of Congress Cataloging-in-Publication Data
Rustad, Martha E. H. (Martha Elizabeth Hillman), 1975–
     Sea turtles / by Martha E. H. Rustad.
     p. cm.—(Ocean life)
     Includes bibliographical references (p. 23) and index.
     ISBN 0-7368-0859-0
     1. Sea turtles—Juvenile literature. [1. Sea turtles. 2. Turtles.] I.Title. II. Series.
QL666.C536 R87 2001
597.92'8—dc21
                                                                      00-009861

Summary: Simple text and photographs present sea turtles and their behavior.

Note to Parents and Teachers

The Ocean Life series supports national science standards for units on the diversity and unity of life. The series shows that animals have features that help them live in different environments. This book describes sea turtles and illustrates how they live. The photographs support early readers in understanding the text. The repetition of words and phrases helps early readers learn new words. This book also introduces early readers to subject-specific vocabulary words, which are defined in the Words to Know section. Early readers may need assistance to read some words and to use the Table of Contents, Words to Know, Read More, Internet Sites, and Index/Word List sections of the book.

Table of Contents

Sea turtles live
in the ocean.

Sea turtles are reptiles.

Sea turtles have a shell.

Sea turtles have a beak.

flippers

Sea turtles have
four flippers.

Sea turtles can swim quickly.

Female sea turtles lay
eggs on land.

Young sea turtles hatch from eggs.

Young sea turtles crawl
to the ocean.

Words to Know

beak—the hard part of a turtle's mouth; turtles do not have teeth.

egg—a case in which a young bird or reptile grows; female sea turtles lay as many as 200 eggs in a nest.

female—a person or animal that can give birth or lay eggs

flipper—a flat limb with bones on a sea animal; sea turtles use four flippers to swim.

hatch—to break out of an egg; young sea turtles hatch only at night.

quickly—very fast; some sea turtles can swim up to 6 miles (10 kilometers) per hour.

reptile—a cold-blooded animal with a backbone; most reptiles lay eggs.

shell—a hard outer covering; unlike most turtles, sea turtles cannot pull their head, flippers, and tail into their shell for protection.

swim—to move through the water; sea turtles must swim quickly to escape predators.

Read More

Jay, Lorraine A. *Sea Turtles.* Our Wild World. Minnetonka, Minn.: NorthWord Press, 2000.

Johnston, Marianne. *Sea Turtles, Past and Present.* Prehistoric Animals and Their Modern-Day Relatives. New York: PowerKids Press, 2000.

Lepthien, Emilie U. *Sea Turtles.* A True Book. New York: Children's Press, 1996.

Internet Sites

AquaFacts—Sea Turtles
http://oceanlink.island.net/aquafacts/seaturtle.html

Sea Turtle Printout
http://www.EnchantedLearning.com/subjects/turtle/Seaturtlecoloring.shtml

Sea Turtles
http://www.seaworld.org/Sea_Turtle/seaturtle.html

Turtle Beach
http://www.discovery.com/exp/turtles/turtles.html

Index/Word List

Word Count: 50
Early-Intervention Level: 7

Credits

Steve Christensen, cover designer and illustrator; Kia Bielke, production designer; Kimberly Danger, photo researcher

Dave Fleetham/Tom Stack & Associates, 1
GeoImagery/Hartlove, cover
Jay Ireland & Georgienne E. Bradley, 4, 6, 10, 12, 18
PhotoDisk Inc., 8
Norbert Wu/www.norbertwu.com, 20
Norman Owen Tomalin/Bruce Coleman Inc., 14
Ron and Valerie Taylor/Bruce Coleman Inc., 16